A Study of Select Plays of Rabindranath Tagore

By

Vivek Vishnupant Joshi

Content

Chapter I

Introduction

Chapter I

Introduction

Rabindranath Tagore, a man of versatile genius and achievements was the first Indian writer who gained for modern India a permanent place on the world literary map. He mainly wrote in Bengali and translated his own creations into English, often changing, transforming the originals thus his English renderings may be called trans-creations.

Rabindranath Tagore was born at Jorasanko, Calcutta (Now Kolkata) on 6th May 1861. His grandfather, Prince Dwarkanath Tagore, was an intimate friend of Raja Rammohan Roy, a great thinker and social reformer. He was practical man of affairs and lived lavishly. His eldest son, Debendranath, was sedate and thoughtful. He joined the Brahma Samaj and avidly read the Upanishads. After his father's death he had to administer the entire *Zamindari* but he avoided chicanery and fairly and squarely managed all affairs. It was due to his uprightness that he was known as Maharshi, the great sage.

Rabindranath Tagore was born in a home teeming with creative activities. He wrote, he sang, he acted and he poured himself out on every side. In the Tagore family the East and the West met under the influence of his grandfather Prince Dwarkanath Tagore, who had introduced European painting, western furniture, Italian status and western manners. Despite these influences his family did not lose its sanctity and continued to observe the religion of the *Upanishads.*

Rabindranath Tagore's birth coincided with the dawn of Indian renaissance which found expression in three different movements- religious, literary and national. He was deeply influenced by these movements. The religious movement was introduced by Ram Mohan Roy who did his best to establish spiritual values, lost in the mire of old traditions. Bankim Chandra Chatterjee, who was the pioneer of the literary movement, liberated literature from stagnation and the lifeless and empty vaunt of rhetoric. Madhusudan Dutt and Dinbandhu Mitra were other stalwarts of literary renaissance in Bengal. Madhusudan Dutt renovated Bengali poetry by imparting to it fresh vigour and ease, flexibility and spontaneity.

Dinbandhu Mitra wrote his plays on homely themes and in homely speech. The national movement gave Indians a voice to assert their personality. These three currents of Indian Renaissance influenced Rabindranath Tagore's personality and found superb expression in his creations. It is need to mention that the rarest honour for Rabindranath Tagore being a creative writer was that Jana Gana Mana, the National Anthem of this country is written by him.

Rabindranath Tagore began his literary career by writing in Bengali. *Banaphul* is his first verse narrative. When he came back from England, he found himself in Bengal which had been dominated with new ideas and a new spirit in religion, literature and politics. He emerged on the literary horizon to create a new art, new standard and new values. Rabindranath Tagore made memorable beginning as a dramatist with his *Prakritir Pratishodh – Sansyasi* in English. Towards the closing years of the nineteenth century, Rabindranath Tagore had emerged as a talented young creative writer who was giving realization to his perceptions in the form of poetry, drama and fiction.

In 1884 he became the secretary of *Aadi Brahma Samaj* and condemned the Hindu caste system and other orthodox customs. During this period he cultivated closest communion with nature and acquired knowledge of the joys and sufferings of human life. The partition of Bengal in 1905 stirred the conscience of Rabindranath Tagore and he rose to the accession. All his writings of this period are suffused with patriotic vigour. In his essays Rabindranath Tagore criticised the false beliefs and practices of Hindu society. *Sacrifice - Visarjan* in Bengali is one such play in which Rabindranath Tagore strongly criticises the inhuman custom of killing living being in the name of worship.

Rabindranath Tagore is the most celebrated personality in modern Indian literature, popularly called 'Gurudeva' ("Revered Guru") and respected as a visionary. An icon of Bengali culture, he influenced writers in all Indian languages, as well as many Western authors. He became the first non-European to receive the Nobel Prize for Literature in 1913. He wrote prolifically in Bengali, and translated some of his own work into English (these translations are thus considered original work by some critics), while also penning occasional prose in English. The sheer range and variety of his creative output made him most different.

Born into an upper-class Bengali family in Calcutta in 1861, Rabindranath resisted institutionalized schooling. He never completed formal education at any level. However, he showed literary talent quite early—he composed his first poem at the age of eight, and had a poem published when he was 14. He married in 1883, and from 1890 spent a long period supervising the ancestral estates in East Bengal (now Bangladesh), which awakened his love of nature. In 1901 he moved to Shantiniketan in West Bengal, where his father used to retreat for meditation. The starkly beautiful rural setting inspired him to start an open-classroom school there. He suffered several personal bereavements from 1902 to 1907: his wife, father, a son, and a daughter died. Tagore's works reveal a pronounced spirituality from this point, while his nationalist political activism also decreased. In 1910 Macmillan (London) printed his first book of self-translations, *Gitanjali*, which earned him the Nobel Prize for Literature, making him an instant international celebrity. Invitations to lecture poured in, and he toured worldwide for the rest of his life. In 1918 he founded a humanistic university, Vishva-Bharati, at Shantiniketan; in 1922 he established the neighbouring Sriniketan, a village reconstruction centre. He died in Calcutta in August 1941.

Rabindranath Tagore published nearly 60 volumes of poems. In his 13 novels and nearly 100 short stories (a genre he introduced in Bengali), Tagore analysed socio-political problems realistically. He constantly interpreted East to West driven by his credo of 'universal man', based on mutual understanding and cooperation.

Tagore wrote around 50 plays, encompassing every dramatic idiom, from verse tragedy to farce, from symbolic allegory to historical realism. He created several forms new to Bengali, such as musical drama—an operatic mode for which he composed scores from start to finish—and plays about specific seasons, celebrating the cyclical advent of natural phenomena. Late in life, he introduced his brand of dance-drama (*Chitrangada*, 1936; *Chandalika*, 1938), which he choreographed, eclectically using stylized techniques from Indian and South East Asian dances. As his own director, and often lead actor, he stressed the imagination and opposed illusionism or spectacle. He took to painting seriously in the 1920s, and exhibited his strikingly individualistic artworks in Europe.

For a long Rabindranath Tagore's plays were taken to be plays essentially for the *closet* or a *chamber play* – "a play written to be read not to be performed" (1). Rabindranath Tagore' s plays fall into three major groups; the earliest, non-symbolic, of which Sacrifice, Chitra and Malini are the significant ones, second group is of short dramas based on Sanskrit heroic stories and the third one is the drama in long prose those are symbolical. This growth of his career as a literary artist brought him into line with the modern men of the letters of the world. In these plays the very breath of this land and the taste of the real life have found dramatic expression. Rabindranath Tagore spoke frequently on the forces of Brahmanism, of Hindu orthodoxy. At the same time Rabindranath Tagore hailed the universal love taught by Gautam Buddha. He was Brahmin by cast but at the same time he was a son of a Hindu reformer. Rabindranath Tagore's choice of Hinduism was particularly limited to his liking and admiration of the philosophic wisdom of the *Upanishads* and heritage of Sanskrit.

The plays of Rabindranath Tagore are great for its poetry. Bishu sings very meaningful songs;

> Bishu (sings).
> Boatman of my dreams,
> The sail is filled with a boisterous breeze
>   and my mad heart sings
> to the lilt of the rocking of thy boat,
> at the call of the far away landing. (2)
>
>   &
>
> Bishu (sings).
> Mow the corn of the last harvest,
>   Bind it in sheaves.
> The remainder, let it return
>   as dust unto the dust. (3)

In another remarkable play for its musical and poetic genius The Cycle of Springs, Rabindranath Tagore presents his gifted qualities;

> The Minstrel (sings)
>   Victory to life, to joy, to love,
>   To eternal light.
>   The night shall wane, the darkness shall vanish,
>   Have faith, brave heart. (4)
> The Cycle of Springs concludes on the hope for the revival,
>   April is awake.
>   Life's shoreless sea

is heaving in the sun before you.
All losses are lost,
and death is drowned in its waves.... (5)

Red Oleander concludes with this song;

Hark 'tis Autumn calling, -
Come, O come away!
The earth's mantle of dust is filled with ripe corn!
O the joy! The joy! (6)

Dramatic and gorgeous passages are there in his plays. The later plays exposed an elevated approach in the direction of life and disclose a mind moving on the highest planes of thought and feeling.

Through his characters he presented before the audience the range of his mind. His ideas are often reflects in the dialogues and the action of the stage.

Amal: No, I would rather go about and see everything that there is. (7)

Amal: Then I suppose no one has ever been there! Oh, I do wish to fly with the time to that land of which no one knows anything. (8)

Amal: How I wish I were a bird! Then – (9)

In Red Oleanders Nandini reflects the author's mind too often;

Nandini: The Gods have all eternity for their worship, they're not pressed for time. But the sorrows of men cannot wait. (10),

and the King Govinda's realisation in *Sacrifice*,

Govinda: God's words are ever ringing in the world, and he who is wilfully deaf cannot hear them. (11)

the king is replying to the revelation of the plan to kill him;

Govinda: ....For a man loses his humanity when it concerns his gods....... Mother, those who are weak in this world are so helpless, and those who are strong are so cruel. (12).

Reformist Rabindranath Tagore is speaking through Jaising when he is talking to Aparna;

Jaising: .... Do you miss some god, who is god no longer? But is there any need of God in this little world of ours? Let us be fearlessly godless and come closer to each other. They want our blood. And for this they have come down to the dust of our earth, leaving their magnificence of heaven. For in their heaven there are no men, no creatures, who can suffer. No, my girl, there is no Goddess. (13)

Surprisingly surpassing the Aristotelian theory, the plays of Rabindranath Tagore have their own way of stirring emotions. Rabindranath Tagore achieve this by the friendliness of the simple world which Amal's childish purity and eagerness gathers about. However one can mark the playwright's highest power as a dramatist in his short plays.

The study of Rabindranath Tagore's plays recapture life itself. The variety of these plays is remarkable. While translating from his original Bengali, Rabindranath Tagore made extensive changes in the text. These plays are almost 'Trans-created' rather than simple translation. Though the original Bengali plays follow the Elizabethan mode, the English plays are compact and have neat structure. He went on trying his hand at different things, testing various models in his creative work. Krishna Kripalani rightly point out this zeal of the dramatist, for the different in his biography,

"--- he never ceased to experiment- it was not because he had not found his form but because there is no end to this discovery." (14)

A great change was taking place within the dramatist. Beside a desire to serve the people whom he loved, he yearned for the Absolute. His mind was full of musings and longing for the spiritual life.

Rabindranath Tagore's longings are reflected in Amal's speech;

Amal: Oh, I will walk on, crossing so many streams, wading through water. Everybody will be asleep with their doors shut in the heat of the day and I will tramp on and on seeking work far, very far. (15)

This same note is found in Chitra also;

Chitra: ....Now teach me thy lessons; give me the power of the weak and the weapon of the unarmed hand. (16)

It was in this frame of mind and spirit that the Bengali *Gitanjali* was composed in 1909-10. It was followed by *The Post Office* in 1911.

In May, 1912 Rabindranath Tagore went to England with the English translation of the *Gitanjali.* In London he came in contact with G.B. Shaw, H.G. Wells, Galsworthy, Andrew Bradley, Robert Bridges, W.B. Yeats, Ezra Pound and some other celebrities. It was here that Rabindranath Tagore met C.F. Andrews for the first time. He became the dramatist's life long companion and later on joined the teaching staff of Shantiniketan. W.B. Yeats greatly admired the English translation of the *Gitanjali*. The India Society published it with an introduction by Yeats. In November, 1912, Rabindranath Tagore went to America where he lectured at many places. In 1913 Rabindranath Tagore was awarded the Nobel Prize for literature for the English translation of *Gitanjali*. He was greatly honoured wherever he went. An honorary doctorate was conferred on him by Calcutta University in the same year. In 1914 he was knighted. The *Gitanjali* and *The Post Office* marked a great transition in his life when the poet's national longings merged in the universal. Nationalist Rabindranath Tagore was very much shocked by Jallianwallah Bagh massacre and in protest he renounced knighthood.

In 1922 he published his famous play *Raktakarabi*, translated into English as *Red Oleanders*. In 1940 Rabindranath Tagore received from Oxford University the degree of D.Litt. in a special convocation held at Shantiniketan. On August7, 1941 Rabindranath Tagore breathed his last.

For Rabindranath Tagore, his writing was something different. It was not mere act of entertainment; he selected it to express himself, while writing his plays or other creative work Rabindranath Tagore used to enjoy the process of the creation. He was in true sense extracting in purpose of rasas. For *Rasa* could be said to be a two-fold experience felt by the creator and his expression through his art and the experience of the reader (*Sahradayas*) who receive the art. The creator undergoes an emotion and is so overwhelmed by it that he seeks a medium for the expression of his feelings. The reader receives this emotion through the creator's medium and thus undergoes the emotion felt by the creator. Thus the word 'Rasa' is once again created by the creator and then is re-created by the reader.

Thematically the plays fall into two groups: thesis plays and psychological dramas. *The Cycle of Spring, Chitra, Sacrifice* and *Red Oleanders* are thesis plays.

Rabindranath Tagore follows the prescriptions suggested by Bharata in his treaty on the drama, *Natya Shastra*

The *Natya Shastra* was written by the sage Bharata who, it is claimed, was directly inspired by the god Brahma. It is believed to have been written during the period between 400 BC and 200 AD. Some scholars believe it was written by various authors at different times. The text is written in the Sanskrit language, and consists of about 6,000 *sutras*, or verse stanzas, incorporated in 36 chapters. There are some passages that are composed in a prose form. The name can be loosely translated as *The Textbook on Drama*. *Natya* or *Nataka* means drama, and in contemporary usage does not include dance. However, *Nataka* originally derives from the word meaning "dance". This suggests that in traditional Sanskrit drama, music and dancing, as well as acting, were important. Bharata sets out a detailed theory of drama comparable to the *Poetics* of Aristotle. He refers to *Bhavas*, the imitations of emotions that the actors perform, and the *Rasas* (emotional responses) that they inspire in the audience. He argues that there are eight principal *Rasas*: love, pity, anger, disgust, heroism, awe, terror and comedy, and that plays should mix different *Rasas* but be dominated by one.

Here it would not be out of place to see in brief the history of Indian Drama.One of the earliest Indian dramatists was Bhasa whose plays have been inspired by the Ramayana and Mahabharata while Kalidasa was an original playwright who wrote classical plays like *Abhigyan Shakuntalam*, *Kumarsambhavam, Meghadutam* and *Malavikagnimitram*. Kalidasa was the court playwright at the famed Gupta court. He lived at Ujjaini, the capital of the Guptas.

In ancient times the Indian thinking was largely towards searching the truth and depicting the same rather than depend on realism and materialism. It could help in expressing wide varieties of characters and incidents as well as finer emotions. The most renowned and talented dramatists of the ancient era are Kalidasa, Ashwaghosha, Bhasa, Shudraka, Harsha, Bhavabhuti, Vishakadatta, Bhattanarayana, Murari and Rajashekhara who enriched Indian theatre with their works like *'Madhyam Vyayoga', 'Urubhangam', 'Karnabharam', 'Mrichakatikam', 'Uttar Ramcharitam', 'Mudrarakshas', 'Bhagavadajjukam', 'Mattavilasa'* etc.

Historically, the rich style of old classical theatre patronized by the state and the more popular form of theatre supported by people at large got amalgamated and transformed into various local styles in the medieval period due to various socio-political and cultural reasons. Sanskrit rhetoricians distinguish *Kavya* into two kinds: *Drsya* (that which can be seen) and *Sravya* (that which can be heard). In drama, *Drsya* takes predominance over *Sravya*. It is because of its capacity to afford a two-fold pleasure that drama is considered as the best form of literature. Kalidasa, the veteran of Sanskrit drama, says:

> "Sages declare it to be a charming sacrificial feast for the eyes of the Gods. Siva bisected it in his own person which is made one with Uma. Here are seen actions of the world arising from the three qualities (Satva, Rajas and Tamas) and distinguished by various sentiments. Drama, though single, is a manifold entertainment for people of diverse tastes". (17)

The scope of 'Select Plays of Rabindranath Tagore' needs to be explained. The selection includes *Sacrifice* (1917), *Chitra* (1892), *Red Oleanders* (1925), *The Post Office* (1914) and *The cycle of Springs* (1917). Except *The Post office* and *The Cycle of Springs* all the plays are written originally in Bengali and then translated into English by the author himself. *The Post Office* is translated into English by Debabrata Mukhopadhyay. *The Cycle of Springs* is translated jointly by C.F. Andrews and Nishikanta Sen. I have selected these plays for the reasons that, first they all deals with human relationships; secondly the plays propagates philosophic notes and thirdly in these plays Rabindranath Tagore reflect more prominently as a philosopher, reformist and offers possible solutions on the human worries.

*****

References:
1] Mobley J.P. *Dictionary of Theatre and Drama Terms*. Viva Books
   Pvt. Ltd. New Delhi. 1998.
2] P 23, *Red Oleanders*.
3] P 94, *Ibid*.
4] P 489, *The Cycle of Springs*
5] P 519, *Ibid*.

6] P 122, *Red Oleanders.*

7] P12, *The Post Office.*

8] P 23, *Ibid.*

9] P 43, *Ibid.*

10] P112, *Red Oleanders.*

11] P19, *Sacrifice.*

12] P56, *Ibid.*

13] P 66-67, *Ibid.*

14] Kripalani, Krishna. *Tagore, A Life.* National Book Trust, India.
New Delhi 1997. p. 75

15] P15, *The Post Office.*

16] P 8, *Chitra.*

17] Kalidasa, *Malavikagnimitram,* I.4 (Ed. not Known)
(Acquired through oral discussion)

Chapter II

Plot

Chapter II

Plot

Aristotle in his Poetics discussed the concept of plot and suggested two essential parts, *Anagnorisis* (the discovery or recognition scene) (1) and *Peripeteia* (the reversal, usually a reversal in the fortune of the hero.) (2) Both parts serve the purpose of keeping the spectators intact and interested in the proceedings of the play. Anagnorisis part introduces viewers with the characters, issues and a scope of a play. *Peripeteia* is the important part of the drama, since the reversal of the action, twist in the events and other effects occur during this process.

Bharata, renowned author of *Natyashastra*, a treaty on the Indian dramatic theory has also discussed these elements and named as *Adhikarika* (principal) the events which achieve emotions and *Prasangika* (accessory), the scenes serves to inform the spectators about the main plot to enhance the effect. The sequence increases the intensity of the action and in the end arouses the emotions, namely *Pity* and *Fear* in the spectators.

Plot in Rabindranath Tagore's plays could be *Adhikarika* (principal) or *Prasangika* (accessory). The *Adhikarika* plot concerns the primary action and pervades the entire play. *Prasangika* serves to supplement the main topic and relates to subordinate characters other than the chief ones. The plots are firmly rooted in the Indian Ethos and ethics. The plots are not knitted carefully as the prime concern is the music and ideas.

India is one of the few countries which can boast of an indigenous drama, unaffected by any foreign influence. When Hindu plays first became known to the European world through Sir William Jones' translation of *Shakuntala* in 1789, it was then generally thought that Greek literature had penetrated into India, influencing their playwrights; but that opinion does not prevail today. Most critics agree that Hindu drama was neither a borrowing nor an imitation, but the product of native genius.

Aristotle advocates the logical development of six aspects; plot, thought, character, diction, music and spectacle. Every part mentioned in this sequence is equally important for the success of the theatre. The important parameter of the success of the play is the performance on the stage. This performance is specifically presented for the spectators and visual effects supplemented by means of spectacles enrich the enjoyment of the performance.

Rabindranath Tagore has something special in his mind when he deals with some plot. His effort is to re-establish humanity to its pedestal and equate it with Nature and through Nature to divinity. The playwright tries to project human predicament and suggests that it is within the reach of human to cross his/her 'being' and thus become something greater than the lowly self. At the end of *Red Oleanders*, it is not merely the death of Nandini and Ranjan but a complete disorganization in the society is emphasized. A kind of life the diggers lead in Yaksha Town is symptomatic of death-in-life; and by surmounting death Nandini and Ranjan project life-in-death.

Rabindranath Tagore generally follows the Aristotelian model for this play. He follows unities as advised by Aristotle. Rabindranath Tagore's plays are vehicles of ideas. Plays like *Sacrifice* convey a message. Though the plot is secondary part, the issue highlights the play. Theme of *Sacrifice* is a problem of shading of the blood in the name of the God. The massage is conveyed by the playwright by Raghupati's hurling away the image of the Goddess whom he had worship all his life and his acceptance of Aparna and mother in her. The Goddess who is capricious about human falls in the end. A mere stone image of delusion shuts out humanity. Raghupati realises the importance of human love. The beggar girl Aparna makes Raghupati accept the necessity to be human.

The plot of *Sacrifice* has a subsidiary theme as well, the conflict between the Kingly power and the priestly authority, represented by King Govinda and temple priest Raghupati respectively. The King prohibited the shading of blood and priest devotes all his energy to protect the temple from the encroachment of the King. The contradiction that tortures Jaising's life is that he has been taught to believe that destruction is a divine law, but Aparna has made him realise the sacredness of life, of human as well as animal life.

Jaising: ...... Must thou have kingly blood, Great Mother, who nourishest the world at thy breast with life?..... (3)

The conflict between the two is very well portrayed without giving a concrete suggestion. It is left to the audience.

In *Sacrifice* the confrontation between the King and his Queen is placed in different setting. The Queen is aligned with forces of reaction against her husband, the King. The conflict is more dramatic and multi-sided; between husband and wife, between temporal power and priestly authority and between love and duty. The play ends in tragedy and the loss of an innocent life, but in the process the voice of love triumphs and the deity dethroned from the temple finds its true place in the heart of human being.

It is in the light of the theory of Aristotle; an attempt is being made to analysis the plot in the select plays of Rabindranath Tagore. In *Sacrifice*, the main plot is supplemented by the sub plots. The conflict between the King and his Queen; then the King and a priest Raghupati enhances the effect and carry forward the message, the playwright is trying to give. *The post Office* is another play where a boy with his little world of fantasy is presented in a very novel manner. A little boy Amal on account of his illness is forbidden from going out of his room. So he prefers to sit in a window which opens to the roadside. This place offer him a chance to talk with many passers and it is during the discussion with many unknown, a play unfolds the wonder world of a boy. *Chitra* is a story of a girl who is brought up as a boy for the unusual reasons. A play suggests the drastic effects of the unnatural attempts to mould the natural instincts and developments. Chitra can not rely upon her 'training' and pray the Gods to bestow the beauty. Red Oleanders is about the life of the workers who work in utter hopeless situations. Here the workers are diggers in the mines of the gold. A contrast is meaningful since the workers who are digging for the gold; a precious mineral, are not given a fair chance to live a life. In most of the plays the playwright is trying to convey some social message and thus his plays become all the way important in bringing up the issues and concerns of the human life.

Instant impression of the readers, after reading the translations of his plays, though not a lasting one is, that his interest primarily was in morals, philosophy and the social reforms. He has certain ideas to propagate and uses his plays as an instrument for the spread of his convictions. His plays are called the plays of ideas (a play in which the main issue or problem is an intellectual one) (4). The critics includes him with G.B. Shaw for his attempt to voice the social cause and with W.H. Auden for his concern for the miseries of the humanity in this materialistic world. His contribution became more important for the age as the world was caught in the war and the innocents were the victims of the power game of the rulers.

His plays are also known as propaganda plays (a play dealing with a political or social issue and proposing a solution) (5), since the purpose of the dramatist is to make spectators aware of the other side of the reality. His issues are reform in the religion, morality, spiritual development and well being of the humanity. Another name given to his plays is discussion plays. He uses this platform to raise the issues of prime concerns and through his characters discuss the possibilities on the stage.

The Post Office is a play of two acts with a few characters, Amal, Madhav, Sudha, Headman, Watchman, Doctor, Royal Physician, Dairyman and a few boys. The play is about the child's aspiration to live a free life. *Chitra* is one act play with nine scenes. Arjuna, Chitra, Madana, Vasanta and a few villagers are the characters. This play deals with the longings of Chitra for the completeness. *Red Oleanders* is a play in one act. Important characters are Nandini, Kishor, Bishu, Phagulal, Chandra, Professor, Governor, Voice; the King, Headman, the assistants and the diggers in the gold mines. *Sacrifice* is a play with a message. Characters include, Queen Gunavati, Govinda -the King, Raghupati- the priest, Jaising, Aparna, Nakshatra, Ministers and Courtiers. Rabindranath Tagore's faith in religion without the dominance of orthodox outdated customs is reflected in this play. *The Cycle of Springs* (Phalguni- in Bengali) is a long play where cycle of the seasons is a central theme and the characters are symbolic. Chandra - a youth, Kabi Sekara, blind minstrel. The play is very colourful and presents the colourful culture of India in the course of cycles of the seasons.

The basic aim of the dramatist in his drama is the betterment of humanity by subjecting the accepted conventions and institutions to the scrutiny of intellect. His plays are about the social cause, human life which is validated with courage.

In Rabindranath Tagore's plays, there is a conflict of ideas. In Sacrifice some ideas get clashed. The problem of animal and human sacrifice is pitted against the idea of the betterment and development of human life. The dramatist is staunch against the betterment of human life at the cost of living beings.

In his plays Rabindranath Tagore deals with human emotions and actual portrayal of life. With the treatment of human life in the main action the plays of Rabindranath Tagore becomes revolutionary and take the audience to the real life situation and dilemma. The spirits of young people who are eager to strike out on new paths take the plays to a new height. Aparna in *Sacrifice*, Ranjan in *Red Oleanders* and Amal in *The Post Office* are the representatives of the young generation who struggle to throw off the orthodox, out dated inhuman customs. Reformist Rabindranath Tagore is frequently appears in plots. His skilful articulation of plot and subplots brings the effect more positively. The confrontation of the authority of religion and the King in Sacrifice reveals the Tussle. Side by side there is a friction on the home front too. Brother Nakshatra and wife Queen Gunvati are posed against the brother and a husband King. These delicate layers of disagreement create very interesting episodes in the course of the play.

The plot of *Sacrifice* has a subsidiary theme as well, the conflict between the Kingly power and the priestly authority, represented by King Govinda and temple priest Raghupati respectively. The King prohibited the shading of blood and priest devotes all his energy to protect the temple from the encroachment of the King. The conflict between the two is very well portrayed without giving a concrete suggestion. It is left to the audience.

In *Sacrifice* the confrontation between the King and his Queen is placed in different setting. The Queen is aligned with forces of reaction against her husband, the King. The conflict is more dramatic and multi-sided; between husband and wife, between temporal power and priestly authority and between love and duty. The play ends in tragedy and the loss of an innocent life, but in the process the voice of love triumphs and the deity dethroned from the temple finds its true place in the heart of human being.

Equally beautiful is the next play *Red Oleanders* where the King and the Governor who initially shares the camp; departs when realised the futility of the greed. Human aspect is added to the tense when Nandini and Kishor, Nandini and Professor & Nandini and Chandra relationship walks parallel to the main action. Subtle events in a play *The Post Office* are interesting where materialist Madhav and child Amal, both striving for freedom, confronts. Both are aspiring freedom but the idea of it is very in both the personalities.

Transformation is the recurring theme in the plays of Rabindranath Tagore. The king's transformation in favour of non-sacrifice, Amal's transformation from a child to non-existing philosopher, Chitra's transformation from pseudo identity to the existing feminine, the King's transformation from an invisible to the human being- from voice to visible, nature's transformation from winter to summer are the important and significant turning points in his plays. The oppressed diggers, humble Sudha transformed to the courageous protestors who voice against the tyranny. The characters reflect the philosophy of the playwright who speaks about change. The change that is inevitable.

*****

References:

1] Mobley J.P. *Dictionary of Theatre and Drama Terms.* Viva Books
      Pvt. Ltd. New Delhi. 1998.

2] *Ibid.*

3] P 79, *Sacrifice.*

4] Mobley J.P. *Dictionary of Theatre and Drama Terms.* Viva Books
      Pvt. Ltd. New Delhi. 1998.

5] P 79, *Ibid.*

Chapter III

Characters

Chapter III
Character ******** till date 16-04-2018

The characters in the plays of Rabindranath Tagore are drawn from all strata of the society and from different professions. The Kings, Ministers, Politicians, lovers, children and workers. There are conservative as well as progressive characters. Ordinary citizens like diggers, intellectuals like the poets and saint everyone finds place and move across his stage.

Aparna is a simple girl but she proves herself tough to take the society at hard when there is a demand. Nan`dini is also a strong character who compels the King to change his set of mind. Chitra is brought up as a son by her father proved her qualities in pursuance of the goal and wins the blessings from the gods. She gets married with Arjuna despite his vow.

Madhav in *The Post Office* is materialistic and living a life by his own ideas. For him money matters much. Nothing is more important for him. He says to Gaffer: "You know, brother, how hard all this getting money in has been. That somebody else's child would sail in and waste all this money earned with so much trouble – Oh, I hate the idea." (1)

He considers natural beauty as wastage:

> "Now listen, since that hill stands there upright as a barrier, it
> means you can't get beyond it. Else, what was the use in heaping up
> so many large stones to make much a big a bi affair of it, eh! (2)

He proceeds further with his views and on Amal's query about the learned people, Madhav: "No, they don't have time for that sort of nonsense. They are not crazy like you. (3)

When he knows that the King himself is coming to his house to meet Amal he suggests him to ask for a gift:

Madhav (whispering into Amal's ear) My child, the King loves you. He is coming himself. Beg for a gift from him. You know our humble circumstances. (4)

In *The Post Office*, Amal is living in a world of fantasy. He is fascinated by the outer world and long for everything. His thirst for relationship, sharing makes him different and representative of the class who is in search of identity in the materialistic world. He gets attracted with the stories and wants to hear those from Gaffer, Sudha and whoever he came across. He tells Gaffer, "….. and in the evenings she would carry the lamp round the cow-house, and then come and sit by me to tell me tales of Champa and his six brothers.(5)

Gaffer in this play in disguise of Fakir tells Amal the stories about mysterious land and the child is overwhelmed by the description:

Amal: Tell me, Fakir, what the Parrots' Isle is like.

Gaffer: It's a land of wonders: it's a haunt of birds. No men are there; and they neither speak nor walk, they simply sing and they fly." (6)

Amal have lost his parents and in imagination feels their presence:

Amal: I feel that mother and father are sitting by my pillow and speaking to me. (7)

Sudha in this play represents love and affection. She is a daughter of the flower-seller and used to share her part in the household. Thus while collecting the flowers for making the garlands Sudha collects the insight about the life. Though she is just a small kid, she perfectly understands the mind of Amal and assures him the flowers 'on her return'.

Nandini in *Red Oleanders* who symbolises joy in the adverse situation is a significant character. In Nandini, Rabindranath Tagore visualises the alternative to the evils in the civilization.

The King in this play is another character which materialise the dramatist's faith that if a person is ready to accept and change for a good cause, a life can be meaningful. When the King comes in contact with Nandini, he realises the shortcomings and futility in his life. He says,

King: Be brave Nandini, trust me. Make me your comrade to-day. (8)

She makes him realise that he has imprisoned in the wrong and narrow notions of greatness and thus have spoiled himself. The shift in the character reflects the dramatist's concept of human life and strengthens the faith in spiritual aspects of living.

The characters like Raghupati in *Sacrifice*, Madhav in *The Post Office* and the Governor in *Red Oleanders* represent the old accepted hierarchy, order and the set principles those govern the system. They work as the protector of these folds. Raghupati is very adamant about the rights of his caste and the superiority of his priesthood;   Raghupati: the worship offered by the most ragged of all beggars is

> not less precious than yours, Queen. But the misfortune is that Mother
> has been deprived. The misfortune is that the King's pride is growing
> into a bloated monster, obstructing divine grace, fixing its angry red eyes
> upon all worshipers. (9)

While these two camps are all set to protect their interests there is a third camp also, which is most of the time in the dilemma. This camp can not firmly decide as to what its choice should be. As a matter of fact, a human King, in *Sacrifice* confronts with religion and put ban on the sacrifice of the living being. But the administrator in the King can not allow him to let his kingdom go out of his control. This dilemma is very intricate and interesting feature of the plays of Rabindranath Tagore.

The same conflict in *Red Oleanders* tests the King when after listening to the woes of the working class he shows some positive changes in his mentality and is confronted with his own administration. The King says;

King: Yes, my fight is against them. (10)

Another play *"The Cycle of Springs"* is very interestingly features the change in the attitude.

Rabindranath Tagore put women on a high pedestal. It is found that women are the initiators of action in the selected plays. Nandini want to talk to a 'Voice'. This is the turning point of the play, *Red Oleanders;*

Gosain: Whom are you prodding like that?

Nandini: That boa-constrictor of yours, who remains in hiding and swallows men. (11)

There are many noteworthy women characters in his plays. They are modern by thought yet not willing to go completely against the set system. Nandini, Aparna, Sudha and Chitra are the trendsetters for the generation.

Sudha, Aparna, Chitra, Nandini, Chandra and Gunavati are the representatives of the women in general. They have their own concepts of life. Though aggressive, Nandini is typical woman who waits for her dear one;

Nandini: When Ranjan comes he'll see I am waiting for him. (12)

They are very common characters in the sense that they live in a set pitch and with their own speed. The things changed when there is a disturbance. Aparna's life is monotonous and unnoticed. It is the sacrifice of her loving goat in the temple of the Goddess Kali that brings her to the front and makes her voice loud enough to compel others to listen. She is bold enough to speak her mind;

Aparna: Mother has taken? It is a lie. Not mother but demon. (13)

Chitra's realisation of her womanhood changes her attitude and she demands the attributes of woman from the Gods, Vasanta and Madana.

Sudha in *The Post Office*, Chitra in *Chitra*, Nandini in *Red Oleanders* and Aparna in *Sacrifice* are the major characters which set the ball rolling. They are reformists, rebel and modern by thought, relationship and action. These characters are the driving force in the plays.

Nandini is more aggressive and firm in her course of action. The tussle between the King and the commons is multi faceted. The ruling circle and the follower's circle are very interesting camps in the plays of Rabindranath Tagore.

Rabindranath Tagore introduces action, but surprisingly it does not spring naturally from character and plot, it is introduced to keep the play moving. The reason may be that he was not primarily interested in action. He was more interested in the discussion and the flow of ideas. He was interested in the characters only as vehicle of ideas. They are the spoke persons of the dramatist. The characters speak the mind of the playwright. Aparna voices against the sacrifices and make the movement against the religious orthodoxy more powerful and effective. His attempt was an artistic effort to help the cause put forth by Raja Ram Mohan Roy in Bengal.

Rabindranath Tagore's characters are types. They represent the human being around. The vehicles of ideas, as they are, most of these characters move unintentionally. They are forced to behave the way they are moving. Raghupati in *Sacrifice* symbolically represent the fundamentalist's set of mind. The King in *Red oleanders* represents the human civilization. His aspirations are the reflections of the reflections of the human aspirations in the materialistic world. Amal is a representative of the class of people in search of salvation (*Mukti*) and waiting for the saviour. Kabi Sekara represents the seer showing the right path to the baffling generation. Chitra is none other but a symbol of the generation, totally confused about the goals of the human life and its meaning. She is in search of totality and aspires for the divine help and some solace.

Aparna personify the life force and advocates the humanitarian point of view. Her protest against the living sacrifice is something more than the mere act of the rejection of the age old customs. She voices the reformists and a goat which got killed suddenly becomes a symbol of the 'oppressed'. One can easily relate the theme of the plays of Rabindranath Tagore to the political movements the country was involved with, if is aware of the social and political milieu of his period.

*****

References:
1] P 8, *The Post Office*.
2] P12, *Ibid*.
3] P13, *Ibid*.
4] P 57, *Ibid*.

5] P 44, *Ibid.*

6] P 42, *Ibid.*

7] P 56, *Ibid.*

8] P 114, *Red Oleanders.*

9] P 30, Sacrifice.

10] P 117, *Red Oleanders.*

11] P 103, *Ibid.*

12] P 59, *Ibid.*

13] P 16, Sacrifice.

Chapter IV

Style

Chapter IV

Style

Rabindranath Tagore evinces greater interest in poetic presentation of his ideas than in considering the theatrical aspects of his plays. Rabindranath Tagore can ably dramatize ideas like relation between Nature and the human. It is found that even if his ideas are thought provoking he makes his presentations mostly poetic, which does not fully meet the demands of the stage. He makes frequent references to the socio-political consciousness. The symbolism in the play "has an unambiguous anti-establishmentarianism." (1) Through this playwright weaves an artistic pattern that is in the contrast of each other and at the same time unique.

Since the English Literature of this age was greatly influenced by Shakespeare a new prose style was developed. G. P. Deshpande calls it, "Anglo-native prose-style". (2) Long flowing sentences, ornate speech and liberal use of Sanskrit were some of the specialities.

Initially the plays of Rabindranath Tagore were taken to be plays essentially for the *closette* or a *chamber play* (a play written to be read not to be performed) (3). With the time and the increasing no. of the performances this notion was proved wrong.

In the plays of Rabindranath Tagore the characters and the action are subordinated to the ideas which constitute the dramatic theme. In most of his plays Rabindranath Tagore try to focus on the struggle between the individual and the state, between the liberate impulse and the compulsive will. Dramatic conflict in Red Oleanders is half allegorical and half realistic. The adverse effect of the development and the scientific technique on the relationship between the individual and social, intelligence and the intellect is prominently highlighted in his plays; *Red Oleanders* is an important play, which shows Rabindranath Tagore at his best. Rabindranath Tagore very clearly highlights the desired changes to overcome the complexities of the human life. The solutions are suggested in dramatic form.

The King in *Red Oleanders* has come out of his 'world' and become one with the forces of life represented by Nandini. The dichotomy between life force and customs finds a metaphorical adaptation. Rabindranath Tagore emphasis the Hindu philosophy frequently when he suggests that death is not the end; but a new beginning and there may be another life after death. When Bishu asks Phagulal as to where Nandini has gone, his reply is metaphoric;

Phagulal: To the last freedom. (4)

The dark chamber of the 'unseen' King is another symbolic representation of man's imprisonment in his own concept s of worn-out customs, which Rabindranath Tagore refers elsewhere as 'the dreary desert sand of dead habits.'

Rabindranath Tagore uses number of objects, images, words as the symbols. Plays serve different purpose for him. Playwriting is not mere a profession or entertainment for Rabindranath Tagore. His plays are the vehicle of his ideas. His selection of the theme and the characters often attracts the viewers and the readers.

The effect of his plays is two fold. First one is an instant and the fascinating. This comes with the reading or viewing of the play. Second effect comes with the association and the meaning that get added to the understanding with the time. Among the huge selection I restricted up to just five plays, obviously for the practical limitations on my part and for the scope of this study. It is really a giant task to study all the aspects and stylistic features of Rabindranath Tagore in the small attempt like this one. Still I can assure that the best of my attempt was made.

The *Post Office* is a different play and in this play playwright advocates the liberty. On surface the issue is about the child Amal's fancy to move out of his house. But the dramatist adds very subtle notes to this seemingly simple plot. This is very fascinating style of Rabindranath Tagore and with the child's longing for freedom he attached his concept of liberal human life. He propagates the freedom to the children. The symbolic use of window and doors as the entry points of the new thoughts and liberation is very dramatic in this play. Thus Madhav in his attempt to save Amal from the weather close all the doors and windows. He is not very happy to do this;

> Madhav: No, I've used the utmost care, never let him out of doors; and
>
> the windows have been shut almost all the time. (5)

The play centres round a child Amal's thirst for freedom from the captivity as Madhav due to the ill health of Amal wants to protect a child. Interesting twist in the play is Madhav who is an obstacle in the so called freedom of Amal, he think that he is a victim of a child's responsibilities. A play opens with the dialogue;

> Madhav: What a state I am in! Before he came, nothing mattered; I felt so
>
> free. (6)

Both these points of view are very ably put forth by Rabindranath Tagore. The playwright gives universality to the characters with his style. His Post man is nobody else but, as he suggested, the God who sends divine messages to everyone to be distributed through 'the post office'.

> Amal: Do letters come from the King to this office here?
>
> Watchman: Of course. One fine day there may be a letter for you in
>
> > there.
>
> Amal: A letter for me? But I am only a little boy.
>
> Watchman: The King sends tiny notes to little boys. (7)

Rabindranath Tagore loved to make life and natural forces play great part in the play. The urge for liberation of human being in domestic, moral and spiritual field was supported by the desire for liberty in social life.

Aparna's crusade in *Sacrifice* for her goat reflects the author's wish to protect the living being against the ill-treatment. Nandini's striving against the custom and the fate of the oppressed, remind us of the struggle of the social reformers in the state of Bengal. Here Rabindranath Tagore is at his best in not only reflecting the contemporary real life situation, but also in speaking his mind and set the ball rolling.

The search of the in-depth intricacies of the human mind happened to be the major effort of the playwright. The Queen Gunavati of *Sacrifice* is desperate for a child. She tries every way out to get a one. She is ready to offer a blood in worship if it is going to please the Goddess Kali. Nandini in *Red Oleanders* is another character from this aspect. Her plight for the rescue of the diggers in the Yaksha Town and the tussle in the mind, whether to opt for the reforms or to live happily with Ranjan, both are very effectively reflected in the play.

Easy and simple Diction: Rabindranath Tagore had great command over English and he artistically used it for expressing his spiritual vision and deep mystical feelings. His words are easy, simple and highly suggestive. His style is full of colloquial idiom. He employs apt and simple vocabulary to communicate deep spiritual feelings. Felicity and melodious ness of expression are the cardinal features of his style. Words like 'lotus', 'life', 'death', 'sun' are found in abundance. Words evoke pictures of the nature, landscapes, birds, and animals, seasons and the great elemental powers, like the sun, the moon etc. He uses delicate and colourful vocabulary in describing human beauty and grace. He uses easy and simple words which enable him to create the familiar atmosphere.

Archaisms : The use of archaisms like 'thee' , 'thou' imparts antique flavour to Rabindranath Tagore's diction and reveals the dramatist's ardent yearning for complete identification with the theme he is dealing with.

Gunavati: Have I offended thee, dread mother? (8)

Picturesque and colourful vocabulary: Rabindranath Tagore employs a highly colourful and picturesque vocabulary to express effectively spiritual concepts. The contrast between simple and great, known and unknown is dealt very effectively. His language is close to the everyday language. There are very few less known words. He uses short words which are significant both for their sense and their sound. Rabindranath Tagore's style is marked by felicity of expression, classical simplicity and austerity which add to loveliness and majesty.

Imagery and symbolism: Imagery is all pervasive in Rabindranath Tagore's creative writing and it gives a kind of unity to it. Image is 'an expression evocative of an object of sensuous appeal. It usually serves to make an impression more precise it may, on the other hand, carry the mind from too close a dwelling on the original thought.' (9) Rabindranath Tagore's style is distinguished by the use of numerous beautiful images, romantic metaphors and suggestive symbols which are worth noting for their depth, beauty, exotic freshness and sheer creative beauty. It gives concrete expression to the dramatist's emotions and contributes to the charm of his art that is already illustrative, decorative, evocative and emotive. It imparts clarity, picturesque ness and correctness to his thought and experience.

Rabindranath Tagore's imagery is mainly drawn from the following sources:

Nature: Imagery like flowers, seasons and river. There are countless references to common objects of nature and to common people. The imageries those the dramatist frequently uses are, Indian seasons and the beggars. Nature-imagery is expressive of playwright's intense love of nature and his minute observation of its beauties and charms. It also imparts a pastoral touch and freshness to his poetry.

Indian Classical Mythology: Indian classical mythology greatly influenced Rabindranath Tagore and he derived most of the images in his work from it. *Chitra, The Cycle of Spring* and several other plays are full with the imageries from mythological sources. His Nobel Award winning *'Gitanjali'* is heavy with the images from mythology. The Vaishnava poets and the *Gita* provided Rabindranath Tagore a rich and varied treasure of imagery. Deeply influenced by the mythological books Rabindranath Tagore thinks that the human body is the temple of the soil, the human soul is the temple of God.

Inner conflict in the mind of a character and the outer conflict on the stage become important sources of the presentation. Normal words are not sufficient to express the inner conflict and ideas which are quite inexpressible. This may be the reason why the dramatist opted for the use of symbols in his plays like a goat, in *Sacrifice*, Madana, in *Chitra*, the diggers, in *Red Oleanders*.

Red flowers in both the plays *Sacrifice* and *Red Oleanders*, frequent use of the different flowers in his plays shows his love for the Nature and his sense of beauty. Flag-staff in Red Oleanders and the idol of the Goddess Kali in Sacrifice, both symbolises the supremacy of the authority which is unquestionable. Demolition of these highly sacred symbols by the King and the priest Raghupati respectively, suggests that mental acceptance of the authority can be challenged by heart and the emotions.

Colourful images present vivid imageries. Bishu's description;

Bishu: ....but there's also the *green* of the woods, the *gold* of the sunshine..... (10)

Bishu: To that boundless tavern, underneath the blue canopy? (11)

Use of the unseen social forces as the dramatic personage is another interesting feature of the playwright. The detail analysis was the need why like the playwright Galsworthy, playwright also opted for the characters like the God Madana (Eros) and Vasanta (Lycoris) in his play *Chitra*. Rabindranath Tagore has shown the way of fusing fantasy and reality by bringing these two different sources together. He constantly opted for the experiments in fresh dramatic devices. For him his play are a medium of the expression and the experience. Voice in *Red Oleanders* serves the same purpose. The playwright believes that the purpose of art is expression and interpretation of human life.

Description of unhappy incidents like death, war is reported through the dialogues. When Sudha ask Physician about Amal, he replies;

Physician: Directly the King comes and calls him. (12)

In *Red Oleanders* also the king is reporting a death of Kishor thus:

King: He burst himself against me, like a bubble. (13)

Rabindranath Tagore gives very picturesque description of the characters. Here is an example how a professor describes Nandini:

Professor: She has for her mantle the green joy of the earth. That is our Nandini. In this Yaksha Town there are governors, foremen, headmen, tunnel-diggers, scholars like myself; there are policemen, and undertakers, - altogether a beautiful assortment! Only *she* is out of element. Midst the clamour of the market place she is a tuned-up lyre. There are days when the mesh of my studies is torn by the sudden breeze of her passing by, and through that rent my attention flies away *swish*, like a bird. (14)

His use of ornamental language is noteworthy. Description of the personalities becomes more particular with his proper use of alternatives. In Red Oleanders Nandini is confronting with Voice (King in disguise) in this scene. A Voice asks:

Voice: Has the mid-day sun any companion? (15)

Again the same beauty appears in this scene when Voice praises Nandini:

Voice: On your face, there is the play of life in your eyes and lips; at
the back of you flows your black hair, the silent fall of death. (16)

Rabindranath Tagore's faith in religion, his acceptance of the power of the almighty reflects frequently in his plays. It appears that his characters speak his mind. They accept the reality that there are certain things which are beyond the human control. Again and again the characters turn to the super-powers for the rescue from the tangles of human life. Queen Gunavati in *Sacrifice* prostrates:

Gunavati: ....O Mother Kali, your creation is infinite and full of wonders,
only send a child to my arms in merest whim, a tiny little warm living flesh
to fill my lap, and I shall offer you whatever you wish. (17)

Chitra also in search of completeness turns at last to the God Madana and prays:

Chitra: ......O Love, god Love, thou hast laid low in the dust the vain
pride of my manlike strength; and all my man's training lies under thy feet.
Now teach me thy lessons; give me the power of the weak and the weapon
of the unarmed hand. (18)

Chitra: ...... Therefore I have come to thy door, thou world-vanquishing
Love, and thou, *Vasanta*, youthful Lord of the Seasons, take from my
young body this primal injustice, an unattractive plain-ness. For a single
day make me superbly beautiful, even as beautiful as was the sudden
blooming of love in my heart. (19)

The reformist characters tend to reject the outdated, inhuman customs and yet rely upon the religion. They neither give up nor are ready to accept it in totality and in the present form. Is there any reason to disagree that the reformist Rabindranath Tagore frequently appears on the stage and strive constantly to propagate the spirituality and the purification of the orthodox outdated customs which brings the religion under the severe criticism.

Irony is very striking feature in the plays of Rabindranath Tagore. He presents this device with his speciality. He makes his scenes effective by employing the contrast to the situation. Nandini is waiting to meet Ranjan and presents a garland of *Kunda* to the governor. Governor while accepting the gift has different plan in mind. Dramatist presents both points of view in the same scene. This play is presented in a series of scene. The structure hints at very famous *Yatra* style of dramatic presentation.

Rabindranath Tagore believes in the concept of the ruler who appears frequently in the plays. This ruler is in different attire. Sometimes he is the King, then at other the almighty. Almost in all the plays I have selected for this study, there is a presence of such character which is more than general human being. The role of this ruler is different from place to place. The ruler is generally present and visible but sometimes invisible still referred frequently.

There is no doubt about the capacity of the playwright to use different languages at once. His proficiency in Bengali as well as in English is beyond any question. Surprisingly there are some unusual instances where the dramatist intentionally or un-intentionally places certain structures which sometimes confuse the readers. This unusual pattern often obstructs the smooth proceeding of a play. For instance, Bishu is asking Phagulal:

Bishu: .....What say you, Phagulal? (20)

Or, Nandini's concern for Kishor;

Nandini: Run away, Kishor, do, - back to your work, quick! You'll be
late again. (21)

Nandini: Show it me. (22)

Nandini: ...... But do be careful. (23)

and again Nandini while defending herself,

Nandini: Because I serve no purpose of his. (24)

This unusual sequence is followed in other plays also for example when Amal says,

Amal: To the King! Do, will you?....... (25)

and whatchman replies,

Watchman: Shouldn't talk like that, my child. (26)

Little girl Sudha also is no exception,

Girl/Sudha: Ah me! Don't go then! Should listen to the doctor. (27)

There is another instance of this pattern when boy in a scene ask surprisingly,

Boy: Say, won't you get a scolding for this?   (28)

Or Gaffer's,

Gaffer: Is it so very astonishing? I am like you. A journey doesn't
    cost a thing. I tramp just I where I like. (29)

As Herald report the Royal Physician's arrival to treat a little boy Amal.

Herald: Yes, then. The King sends his greatest physician to attend *on* his
young friend. (30)

There is no surprise then if Rabindranath Tagore remains difficult to understand. On account of his reach imagery, ideas, plots and strange way of presentation he always lead his age.

＊＊＊＊＊

References:

1] Chakravartee, Moutushi. "Myth and Symbol as Metaphor: A Re-
    Consideration of Red Oleanders and Hayavadana".
    The Literary Criterion. Vol.26, No.4, 1991. pp. 31-40.

2] Deshpande, G.P. (Ed.) Modern Indian Drama: An Anthology. New Delhi:
    Sahitya Akademi, 2000. Page xii.

3] Mobley J.P. *Dictionary of Theatre and Drama Terms.* Viva Books Pvt. Ltd.
    New Delhi. 1998.

4] P 103, *Red Oleanders.*

5] P 50, *The Post Office*

6] P 5, *Ibid.*

7] P 25, *Ibid.*

8] P 13, *Ibid.*

9] Shipley, J.T. *Dictionary of World Literary Terms* George Allen and Unwin, London. 1955. Page 219

10] P 26, *Red Oleanders.*
11] P 26, *Ibid.*
12] P 59, *The Post Office.*
13] P 113, *Red Oleanders.*
14] P 71-72, *Ibid.*
15] P 56, *Ibid.*
16] P 62, *Ibid.*
17] P 61, *Sacrifice.*
18] P 8, *Chitra.*
19] P 9, *Chitra.*
20] P 25, *Red Oleanders.*
21] P 1, *Ibid.*
22] P 2, *Ibid.*
23] P 2, *Ibid.*
24] P 11, *Ibid.*
25] P 22, *The Post Office.*
26] P 22, *Ibid.*
27] P 31, *Ibid.*
28] P 36, *Ibid.*
29] P41, *Ibid.*
30] P 55, *Ibid.*

Chapter V

Conclusion

Chapter V

Conclusion

It has been said that Rabindranath Tagore was not successful dramatist. That he had merely use theatre because it gave him a platform to express. He often try to visualise human life which is full with colours, & ups and down, with his set of mind. His spiritual, philosophical personality gets reflected clearly in his plays. It is not always easy for the common audience to understand the intricate, subtle realities, symbolism and the remote references to the human life and the struggle in human mind.

His plays are more than the plays. The purpose of the plays is something high and he goes on serving other purposes like exposition of the measures to correct the orthodox, outdated customs and put forth argument in support of his point of view. Rabindranath Tagore evinces greater interest in the presentation of his ideas than in considering the theatrical aspects of his plays. His ideas though are thought provoking, sometimes does not meet fully with the demands of the stage presentation. Rabindranath Tagore's 'different' voice is hardly heard as effectively as in the other creative forms.

Rabindranath Tagore believed in the reformation. He criticise the outdated rituals. It doesn't mean that he was totally against the religion and faith; rather he as an objective reviewer scrutinise the merits of the *Vedic* methods, philosophy and demerits of the outdated customs. Being the true follower and guided by the sacred *Upanishad*'s teaching, Rabindranath Tagore with three influences namely the reformist movements in his state, the national movement in the course of independence and humanitarian point of view goes on contributing his part in the process of betterment of human life.

A notable exception to the commercial trend was Rabindranath Tagore. Tagore invented a completely new form of indigenous theatre in Bengal. He consciously rejected Western models in favour of open-air productions at his school in Shantiniketan, which he later took on influential tours all over India. His presentational style integrated original music, dance, verse, design, and space in lyrical, often symbolic plays, which he directed and acted in himself. He treated cultural and political subjects as diverse as religious orthodoxy, sexual inequality, environmental issues, the celebration of nature, and spiritual quest.

Rabindranath Tagore has something special in his mind when he deals with some plot. His effort is to re-establish humanity to its pedestal and equate it with Nature and through Nature to divinity. The playwright tries to project human predicament and suggests that it is within the reach of human to cross his/her 'being' and thus become something greater than the lowly self. At the end of Red Oleanders, it is not merely the death of Nandini and Ranjan but a complete disorganization in the society is emphasized. A kind of life the diggers lead in Yaksha Town is symptomatic of death-in-life; and by surmounting death Nandini and Ranjan project life-in-death.

Rabindranath Tagore generally follows the Aristotelian model for this play. He follows unities as advised by Aristotle. Rabindranath Tagore's plays are vehicles of ideas. Plays like Sacrifice convey a message. Though the plot play the secondary part the issue highlights the play. Theme of Sacrifice is a problem of shading of the blood in the name of the God. The message is conveyed by the playwright by Raghupati's hurling away the image of the Goddess whom he had worship all his life and his acceptance of Aparna and mother in her. The Goddess who is capricious about human falls in the end.

A mere stone image of delusion shuts out humanity. Raghupati realises the importance of human love. The beggar girl Aparna makes Raghupati accept the necessity to be human.

The Cycle of Springs personifies the cycle of nature as the journey of human life. Spring follows the summer and thus the cycle rotates from birth to death. The human philosophy finds apt parallel in nature which reminds of, 'if winter comes can summer be far behind.', that the cycle is inevitable. All human being can do is to accept and enjoy the law of nature.

In the last quarter of the 19th century there was the remarkable influence of social problems and the reforms on the stage. Rabindranath Tagore introduce the open air theatre in his another innovative experiment-Shantiniketan. Psychological investigation made his characters more interesting. His plays are the projection of the real life on the stage.

Rabindranath Tagore has not tried much to benefit from the tradition of Indian Classical Drama and the folk stage in spite of his acquaintance with the same. Rabindranath Tagore does not attempt to infer an ancient myth from a contemporary point of view. His non-symbolic plays like *Sacrifice*, heavy with suspense and action are exception and presentable on the stage. Rabindranath Tagore, the embodiment of Indian saintly inheritance assumes the role of an exponent and mediator between the civilizations of the East and the West.

Rabindranath Tagore combined the Indian and the Western traditions to bring a synthesis between them.

Rabindranath Tagore while dealing with his plays in English condenses the text; this may be the reason- English version possesses an economy which the Bengali version is deficient in. The critics are of the view that much intricacy and richness have lost in the process of condensing the plays for the non-Bengali audience.

In his book on Indian Drama in English C. L. Khatri has rightly quoted the quotation of Marjorie Boulton;

"A true play is three dimensional, it is literature that walks and talks before our eyes. It is not intended that the eye shall perceive marks on paper and the imagination turn them into sights, sounds and actions; the text of the play is meant to be translated into sights, sounds and actions which occur literally and physically on the stage. Though often the plays are read in silence, if we are to study the drama at all intelligently, we must always keep this in mind". (1)

Modern Indian theatre was being written in different language-cultures and situational specificities matters as much to this theatre as to the theatre based on the epics like the *Mahabharata* and the *Ramayana*. There is a basic text which seemed to grow, to expand at times to constrict itself in performance. This is an important and natural activity in case of music and dance drama.

Limitations of the Dramatist:

1] The beauty and spontaneity of his language are marred by repetition. One thought, one image is repeated again and again until it creates the effect of monotony and dullness.

2] R. Tagore's creative work is not uniformly good. C. Paul Verghese has rightly pointed out, "there is a certain inequality in his thought and matter."(2)

3] Rabindranath Tagore has failed to solve the problem of fusing dramatic stories with dialogue and sense of good theatre. These are the indispensable ingredients for the success of a play on the stage.

C.P. Varghese's words are very pertinent in this context;

"--- In the meanwhile it is necessary for a proper appreciation of Tagore that his reputation as a predominantly mystic poet should not be over-stressed."(3)

Rabindranath Tagore exploits the medium of drama with unusual effects foe shattering a number of social, political doctrines. The playwright was a combination of the artist and the preacher. He was a playwright with different capacities. He could write, compose music, direct his plays and more than that he also acted in his productions.

Interesting difference between Rabindranath Tagore and the other playwrights is that his plays invoke the imagination to the fullest. This is considered to be the major flaw of 'dram of ideas'.

*****

References:

1] Khatri, C. L. *Introduction to Indian English Drama in English* Indian Drama in English, Book Enclave, Jaipur, 2006. Page 2.

2] Verghese, C.P. Problems of Indian Creative Writer in English. Somaiya Pub. Pvt. Ltd. Bombay. 1971. Page 53.

3] *Ibid*

Bibliography

Primary Sources:-

1] Tagore, R. *Chitra* Macmillan India Ltd., Madras, 1992.

2] Tagore, R. *Sacrifice* Macmillan India Ltd., Madras, 1994.

3] Tagore, R. *The Post Office* Wisdom Tree, New Delhi, 2005.

4] Tagore, R. *Red Oleanders* Rupa & Co. New Delhi, 2002.

5] Tagore, R. *The Cycle of Springs* Collected Poems and Plays of
Rabindranath Tagore. Macmillan India Ltd., New Delhi. 2001.
Pages 439 to 519.

Secondary Sources:-

1] Kripalani, Krishna. *Tagore, A Life.* National Book Trust, India.
New Delhi, 1997.

2] Iyengar, K.R.S. *Indian Writing in English* Sterling Pub. Ltd.
New Delhi, 2002.

3] Naik, M.K. *Aspects of Indian Writing in English* Macmillan Pub. Ltd.
New Delhi, 2004.

4] Rukhaiyar U.S. *Symbolism in Tagore's Play 'The Post Office'* Indian
Drama in English, Dr. Khatri C.L. (Ed.) Book Enclave Pub.
Jaipur, 2006. Pages 57-67.

5] Bennet and Balachandran S. The Encyclopaedia of Nobel Laureates
Literature. Dominant Publishers New Delhi, 2007.
Pages 901-912.

6] Herbert W.P. and Mukherjea N. The Encyclopaedia of World's Great
Authors (Literature) Dominant Publishers New Delhi, 2002.
Pages 2003-2006.

7] Dodiya, Jaydipsinh K. and K.V.Surendran Indian English Drama: Critical
Perspectives. New Delhi: Sarup & Sons, 2000. pp. xi, 121.
1. Indian English Drama: Tradition and Achievement by Saryug Yadav
- P.1-13;
2. The Form of Indian Drama in English: A Few Problems
By P. Hari Padma Rani – p. 14-18;
3. Rabindranath Tagore as a Spiritual Seer with reference to The Cycle of
Spring by R. Radhiga Priyadarshini- p 19-25.

8] Mukar, Nand. Indian English Drama: A Study in Myths. New Delhi:
Sarup & Sons, 2003. pp.viii, 230.
Introduction – p. 1-20; 5. Myths in the Plays of Rabindranath Tagore-p.21-50.

9] Surendran, K.V. Indian Writing: Critical Perspectives. New Delhi:
Sarup & Sons, 2000. pp.vi, 361.

Note: 1. Defining the Other: A Study of Tagore's The Home and the World -p.1-14.

10] Deshpande, G.P. (Ed.) <u>Modern Indian Drama: An Anthology.</u> New Delhi: Sahitya Akademi, 2000. pp. xviii, 754

11] Chakravartee Moutishi. *Indian Plays (Rakta Karabi and Evam Indrajit) in English Translation: Some Aspects* <u>Creative Aspects of Indian English</u> Santinath Desai (Ed.), Sahitya Akademi 1995. pp.97. (page 16 of the introduction)

12] Naik, M.K. *The Winds of Change: 1857to 1920* <u>History of Indian English Literature, A.</u> Sahitya Akademi, New Delhi. 1997. pp. 101-103

13] Vatsyayan, K. *Traditional Indian Theatre.* National Book Trust, India. 2005.

14] Mobley J.P. *Dictionary of Theatre and Drama Terms.* Viva Books Pvt. Ltd. New Delhi. 1998.

15] Elam, Keir. *The Semiotics of Theatre and Drama.* Routledge, New York. 2002.

Soft Sources (internet etc.):-

1] Asiatic Society of Bangladesh (2006), "Tagore, Rabindranath", *Banglapedia* [link accessed Mar.09, 2007].

2] Hjärne, H (1913), "The Nobel Prize in Literature 1913", *Nobel Foundation* [link accessed Mar.08, 2007].

3] Microsoft Encarta in Disk form, 2006©. (Ed.)

Journals and News papers:-

1] Chakravartee, Moutushi. "Myth and Symbol as Metaphor: A Re-Consideration of Red Oleanders and Hayavadana". <u>The Literary Criterion.</u> Vol.26, No.4, 1991. pp. 31-40.

*****

www.ingramcontent.com/pod-product-compliance
Lightning Source LLC
Chambersburg PA
CBHW030105300526
45785CB00019B/2721